THE MOB WITHIN THE HEART

RICK BENJAMIN

WAYFARER BOOKS
BERKSHIRE MOUNTAINS, MASSACHUSETTS

WAYFARER BOOKS

WWW.WAYFARERBOOKS.ORG

Look for our titles in paperback, ebook, and audiobook wherever books are sold.
Wholesale offerings for retailers available through Ingram.

Wayfarer Books is committed to ecological stewardship.
We greatly value the natural environment and invest in conservation.
For each book purchased in our online store we plant one tree.

PO Box 1601, Northampton, MA 01060

860.574.5847 | info@homeboundpublications.com

HOMEBOUNDPUBLICATIONS.COM & WAYFARERBOOKS.ORG

for Margaret

CONTENTS

III

IV

CODA

Acknowledgments

About the Author

About the Press

1745

The Mob within the heart
Police cannot suppress
The riot given at the first
Is authorized as peace

Uncertified of Scene
Or signified of sound
But growing like a hurricane
In a congenial ground.

Emily Dickinson

I

SAVING'S

too strong a word for daylight,
as if turning back or forward
clocks could change what
sun does, come what may.

Same thing with lives,
you might say, cupped
hand holding spider or
bee gestures toward

simply honoring life
not rescuing or setting
it free. No matter.
I've hurt or helped

thousands of creatures
by now, for decades-
worth of homicide &
it's opposite, which isn't

saving but maybe just
noticing we can choose
to hold other lives in
our hands resuscitating

that same old story
by breathing into it
new life.

A REPORT ON THE WEATHER

In a dry season   man-made
marshes dry up   water-birds
find new spots   you dream
harbor-ponds   great blue
herons   egrets   geese skim-
ming surface   a deeper
sleep where   frogs wait
out the heat   spells of
hibernation   under
ground until   next rain
opens throats   tuned to
new baritones   bear-tones'
well-graveled   buried voices
in dried season   sex isn't last
thing in mind &   body but not
first either since   desire signals
simply deeper   longing, winding
beneath belly   heart-ward, mind
zinging out   bee-song hovering over
sweetness   sunlight hitting human
faces most   erotically, tactile touch
first thing   most mornings skin's
so sense-   itzized it sweats into
blossom.   Dry seasons forge
narrower   channels into mind-
streams   threads we can still
some-   how follow through
dense   algae blooms cutting
off our   breathing almost
even be-   fore it gets
started.   None of this
is for a   faint-hearted
soul,   dry season, like
this one.

IF SOMETHING SHOULD HAPPEN

for instance, if plates,
tectonic I mean, should
shift under all that weight

between them, cause earth
to shake into itself & take
everything with it, if roof

above my head should
fall, leaving only stars
&, tonight, a moon we

call thumbnail, if ground
opens to swallow whole
what until now we've found

stable, would I know to stand
up from the table where I've
just served dinner & offer

a toast to life, find the right
rhyme for that moment
of dissolution, say

l'chaim to each guest
I've ever invited in, all
of us clinking our broken

glasses, by which I mean,
hearts, as we fall, face-first

into the next place?

CANDLE-POD ACACIA

Just because someone wants
to devour you doesn't mean
you have to let them. Acacia
senses presence of giraffes
& will send out a certain
sourness to its leaf-tips &

pods to stop them feeding
on their top-most branches.
Better, they can send down-
wind signals to rest
of their kind in any stand,
cough up what's bitter

up-bones skyward. Spirit
resists being eaten when
someone else's hunger
says danger's nearby. Best
to throw off scents from
your darkest places, the ones

that put off even you. Maybe
later you'll be ready for that
new becoming, right when
it takes you in: long-
necked trees
camouflaged

in spots, heads
bowed toward

root of
it all.

I HAVE NO ADVICE

to give unless it is to pay attention to bark
of eucalyptus in rain, big waves breaking

on the central coast of California during
El Niño, unless it is to ask why it is called,

El Niño as if some upper-cased Boy took
charge of the weather, to wonder at all

tsunamis that express crashing
as brokenness, to ask so much

more of ourselves on this planet.

HOW TO MAKE SANTA ANA WIND

Begin on low desert floor
harvesting heat as it rises,

sweeping salt & dirt
through air as it skims

every surface. When it
reaches hills &, later,

mountains let it mix with
cooler heads finding in

friction the fire it needs
to summit them. Later,

get out of the way of deep
drops into valleys, ravines,

through tree-stands too
numerous to count. That

hot breath's been swirling
in your own body, twisting

out in gust-dances whirling
dervishes, trances of half-

heard conversation. &, Don't
be surprised when that song

carried from earth's driest
places knocks everything

& everyone you love down.
You can, it seems, absorb

even these blows, although,
exactly, how, no one knows.

LATE STORM

Wind blows through gutters
groans sounding through
a house like moans coming

inside of it. Percussive roof
in rain, water slapping against
panes of glass, that last sigh

you make before sleep. Try
as I might it never becomes
quite audible, say, longing or

dissatisfaction, the breath
just before the one when
you take sudden action

after afternoons & evenings
of doing nothing. This storm
drops two inches an hour &

if ground's hard & dry enough
rivers will flow where we've
never seen them,

& a crowd of frogs so big
& boisterous you'd think
they'd lived here always,

their loud song in praise
of water drowning out
crickets, even someone's

voice asking, did you turn
out the light downstairs?
Some nights were made

for flames to burn down-
wick, to remember something,
anything, bright to show us

a way. Whether or not
you should go or stay, what
comes next, or which text

holds the answer isn't even
what matters, not with trees
all in tatters, not with fronds

& branches & bark scattered
all about your feet where
something that seemed

solid used to be. So what
if another tree has fallen
down? You're bound

to get up again, hear another
guttural wind blowing clear
through your house, knowing

that it could never have been
kept out.

A FEW OF A NUMBER OF ACCURATE ANSWERS

because the ants, insulted, not
showing their usual hospitality,
emptied the whole damn house,

which they figured, in ways ants
figure, by instantaneous head-to
head-communication— lines

humans mistakenly think of as
mechanized—would also carry
a message but somehow did

not, humans' stock of other
creatures' sophistication once
again underestimated;

because pods & pods of
whales composed the same
song through water many

thousands of miles hoping
some listeners with ears
to oceans' surfaces might

not simply hear songs but
also break the linguistic
code like spies listening

through static to Morse
or some other tapping
of human ingenuity

passing for intelligence
or counter-intelligence
while all usual currents

cluttered with noise, so-
nar, electricity, muddy-
ing the waters a waste

of information no one
seemed to have capacity
to sift though, saving

whales become all of a
sudden, of necessity,
more important than

just listening to what
they were singing: you
are a guest here. This

house does not belong
only to you. & We can
carry it away at any
moment & in any

element if whim or
winds or waves
move us to do so.

BAKER'S BROOK BUTTERFLIES

Skim surface of only one
source, absorb its color
in one stroke— reverse-

chameleon. After trans-
formation, no cocoon in
sight, they brush against

water they've become &
spread dust over some
new surface, where you

can watch wings taking
shape as if from one
artist's hand, a mind

alert to the ephemeral
nature of what's real &
what's not.

DDT PLUMES

emanated from backs
of trucks, exterminated
mosquitoes that might

make us sick. We rode
our sting-rays through
chemical clouds said

to be harmless, sweet
scent of insect-death
clinging to wet t-shirts

like sweat. Only later
did those summers
become dangerous

when it leaked that DDT
we'd breathed in made
for blood-kinship &

could kill us, too:
cost of extinction
spelling out our own

demise. That smell
of clouds evaporating
into cloudless skies

with only the fact
of our burning eyes
to signal difference

between blood sought,
given up, retrieved or
come to harm was also

someone else's hunger,
fierce need, & us taking
our lumps on itching arms.

BEAVERS BUILDING DAMS

It takes a long time to build one
but precision's the key, not rush
to stop water in its tracks not

keeping salmon from leaping out
of their own bodies in order to
spawn a next generation after

many years of bodying forth
through what first felt foreign,
like salt. It is salt, one of you is

saying, &, of course, that's right:
simply beginning in fresh water,
some calm pool or eddy—same as

where your own mother was born
you find yourself— Me, with my
buck-teeth, sharp incisors. I've

never done anything but honor
water, salmon, forging new paths
for flow swim up- or down-river,

no slave to human wants to harness
power any way possible. They say,
big dam project, displacing all

critters & humans who've known
free-flowing rivers, for one example,
as life giving, when twigs & even big

tree-branches were quite enough to
stanch too forceful a flow, to redirect
water to some new place it hadn't

already found on its own. They are
all about the surge of electricity, flow
of new technology, artificial light in

every home. Us, we're still teething
on rapids inquiring into what
wants rush, what softer current,

which trees want most to offer
their own bodies to cross a river
or stream while leaving holes, pockets,

tunnels for others to flow through.
See if I'm right. What's sure is me &
all the rest of the beavers will be here

all night.

AT MASHAPAUG POND

In memory of Mary Oliver

Look, late afternoon
light has turned
the surface of water
into liquid mercury,
disappearing green
algae blooms; a three-
eyed frog hops
down into whatever
it calls home, &
everywhere smells
sweet as sickness.
Harming a body
of water takes
only three things:
to dump what we
call waste, to deny
the life of what
receives it, &
to think it won't
hold you, buoyant,
in its willing &
waiting hands.

AUTUMN, ELWOOD

Morning, a murder
of crows finds one
tree, then others

along the same route.
They'll hound a hawk
to fleeing away from

the nests it's been
trying to plunder,
while I'm safely

under a canopy
reading another
page in shade:

the global strike for
climate change led
by a sixteen-year-old

girl from Sweden,
latest loss of gun-
control in a mosque,

his on-line screed
or plea for help before
that, next government

rollback of every con-
ceivable cap on profit
destroying the planet.

My father always hated
crows, their calls & all
ways they aggressively

got after it. Mornings
they woke him up he'd
claim to want to kill

the whole loud
bunch of them,
but he didn't.

Kundera claimed
the great invasion
of the 20th century

was when crows
came into cities &
that's worth thinking

about: a boisterous
takeover without any
weapons in sight, &

no light shining yet on
their plot to take over,
getting after it only after

we've all departed,
finally succeeded in
making up our own

death-bed. Imagine
their numbers, a sky
darkening with their

many murders, that
deafening sound of
life-affirming calls!

DOG WAKING & WATCHING AT DAWN

His own growl wakes me in half-
light, half-dream, an egret, maybe,
balanced on one leg, some stillness

followed by a slow-stepping move-
ment through high-grassed marsh-
land with little in the way of water

in it this drought-season we call
spring. So now we're both up &
about, too early & also too late

for me to notice what he might
have been seeing through glass
that made that deep-throated

murmur in him come to life,
matched by my own low hum
as I take my first sips of coffee

before the long walk we both
will take this May-gray dawn
as locals call it, marine layer

which may or may not burn
off come afternoon. Swallows
shore up their nests both early

& late, never done with safe-
guarding homes for eggs &,
later, their baby-birds, while

hawks & crows ride up-drafts
nearby, keeping watch for any
opening to come. Don't we all

fear that plundering, that small
voice in us dreading, wondering
what comes next? Too lucky, too

fortunate to believe that what
we're seeing out any window
toward the future can last?

Just like the past it can bring
up a growl of warning, of an
other morning where nearby

steps drew our attention to an
opening in our own life where
someone or something else

waited to enter, uninvited
perhaps, soft-stepping their
way in or out before we even

realized they'd been there.

II

MOST DAYS

This dog doesn't bark
at all, except when two
men other side of a wall

are talking about plants,
native species, invasive
ones, what they think

belongs here & what
doesn't. Out walking
earlier, I smelled wild

fennel, not native to
here, & Cody found
a scent in some fast-

growing ice-plant,
which has taken so
much hold of bluffs

they could collapse
under its weight. Or
maybe its holding

them up. It's so hard
most days to decide
who belongs & who

doesn't. I'm not one
to tell a 200-year old
coastal pine to take a

hike because it's not
indigenous to here, or
say to two generations

of undocumented people.
still carrying with them
in bundles & close to

hearts what defines
them, that they can't
stay either. I walk

around in awe of
ways we've all some
how arrived, been

able to adapt to this
dry & drought-ridden
place, dropping roots,

even as these others
determine to replace
all of us with what

lived here before &,
no matter what they
do, never will again.

IN ONE OF BASQUIAT'S NOTEBOOKS

for Deb & Anna

the artist wrote one line
on a single page, the dog
died, & though absence

of a name made a dog
(her? him?) into a thing
there was also so much

empty space on a lined
page, as if only the title
in such a case mattered

making room for only
the fact of it, the dog
died, giving all the rest

of it over to loss, that
empty feeling you get
when you walk into a

house day after day &
there's no tongue or
tail to greet you, no

jumping up with so
much delight you'd
think your presence

counted. Humans
don't greet you like
that. Is it because

of longevity, time
having its way with
love? A dog's hello's
premised on, time is
short— & tails wag
it out like nobody's

business. What does
it mean when a dog
dies, all of those dog-
days after that one?
I've lost a few
by now. One's

never stopped
slipping her
whole body

under my neck
when I spiked
a high fever &

pneumonia,
another's
bark fills

my dreams,
& this one,
this one,

Cody to us, has so
much joy, so much
sadness in him he's

become kindred
spirit: his whole
body moving to

a beat of gladness
along with this
sadness of feeling

him shy away as
your hand moves
downward to top

of his head, some
early injury, maybe
day after day, only

he knows some-
thing about. He
carries it in his

body, memory
of a bad first
year, or seven

years. I look
into his sad
eyes, at his

still-wagging
tail. No one
is more sad &

glad at the
same time
as he is save

Basquiat, &
you, & me
& that mostly

empty page
in one of his
notebooks—

DOS CABEZAS

bad-ass Basquiat
walks up 2 Andy
says I want 2paint

(in) this Factory, &
Warhol, careless,
says get back 2 me

when you've some
thing to show me.
Then Jean Michel

goes home, quickly
paints their heads
on canvas stretched

on two-by-fives—
60 x 60 facing an
artist, undeniably,

in the color esp.,
though the faces,
too, unmistakable

(the paint's still
wet: it's only been
2 hours). Famous

white artist looks
up at black artist
showing him up,

knows he's also
so much better.
So much 4 real

looking coke &
campbell's soup
cans, as if irony

didn't still feed
the capitalist
mob. Basquiat's

the real deal:
means to bite
hands feeding

him, a genuine
cultural critic:
in this case 2nd

head's
much
better

than
first
one.

FIRST NIGHT-BLOOMING CEREUS

in memory of Ashley Bryan

One feels a shudder
doesn't see it;
petals opening
want to be it.

BEGIN HERE

Waking to a dog shaking
a body out of sleep into
ours, clinking his collar
an alarm. Nothing
this one does comes
to harm: he noses
the world rather than
bites it, rises from
another night happy
enough to be alive
his tail triggers
excitement that
lasts all day.
Me, I'm going to
need a cup of coffee
just to face the news
& if you rub my belly
I might give you a sigh
of contentment. But only
after a while. & only after
that, a smile.

EARLY MORNING LOSS LIST

Blue tiger-eye set in a silver band,
a hand that taught me how to make it,
sleep from too many nights to count.

Consciousness, head-meeting side-
walk concussion knocking out sense.
And that Sycamore, front of the house

I fell from. Small house condemned
by a quake, another house salvaged
to the shifting earth, too many

apartments to count. A childhood
river I never knew was there. Hair
I was too proud of, a city, a state,

the Pacific I have now returned to,
too many lizards to count, desert
tortoises hibernating all winter

in the crawlspace separating earth
from a floor above it. Drinking
deep straight from a creek

knowing your body had never
taken in something so pure,
plants to drought, fruit of one

tree no longer singing in your
mouth, too many rotting figs
to count. Fierce love of a one-

eyed grandma, then her spirit
watching over me, his huge
hands hardened by labor,

softened by successive strokes.
A friend, another friend,
another friend, a family member

until the word, suicide lost its
edge. So many butterflies that
used to migrate here. So many

people that used
to migrate here. So
many people who

knew Goleta, &bluffs
much better than me,
sacred trails replaced

by trails less sacred I walk
each day with a dog who
points like a divining

rod to older ribbons of
packed dirt almost buried
in brush. Too much of that

low brush that is really a
forest canopy called,
chaparral, scrub-oak,

yucca, cypress. Knowledge
of the ways of trees, walking
up mountains, Master Dogen

said, or turning, Mary said,
spirits jumping from body
to body so that old stands

were really running. That
reckless run down-mountain
when body begins to feel

more like spirit. Spirit.
Another spirit. Too
many spirits to count.

CHOOSING A NEW HOME

The last one, back in Rhode Island
was old, at least by some people's
reckoning, over 100 years, built

to last in 1903, which in New
England, of course, means
nothing when it comes to

history. Still, light came
through wavy glass panes,
quarter-sawn steps led up to

the second floor, cast-iron
keys fit into hard-wood
doors, an ice-box meant

to hold blocks instead
of cubes was built into
a wall— & all of this

pleased me to no end.
If you send someone
back to California

where he's from after
three decades he'll
feel out of place with all

the newness: tract-homes,
plants & trees never meant
for the dry space we call

coastal desert, all the other
transplants searching
for something they'll call

paradise. Me, I already
know that there's a certain
price for all that: the earth

shaking whenever it has
a mind too, hill-side sliding
down over roads after hard

rain, Santa Ana winds sparking
fires burning for months
on end. Not to mention a new

house: built just last year, small
by East-coast standards, no
basement for one thing, fake

wood shingles for another,
a few touches that remind you
of arts & crafts, but not really.

Of course it's silly to compare
with a nature preserve out
back, coastal pines,

eucalyptus, sound
of owls & frogs, even
waves finding their way into your

dreams each night. You've
made peace with cheap
construction, thin walls,

dark veneered floors
picking up all the dirt
& dust. Ants come in

through the cracks,
creatures stir all night
out back. In this pre-

fab world you're as close
as you've ever been to
non-human you've

always longed to be.

ELEMENTAL

(One)

I have never met a body
of water I did not want
to tap into— faucet &
basin, cold-snapped
creek-bed covering
stones, or soft moans
of a pond coming un
done early spring on
a colder coast than
this one.

(Two)

doctor of needles said
fire in my liver burned
hot as Santa Ana winds
rising off desert floor &
over mountains gaining
steam, said he'd bring
fever up & out of me in
six weeks, or eight, it
was hard to predict
such heat. By then I'd
witnessed wind spark
something all by itself,
watched flames emanate
from no ember in a state
defined by its degree of

burns. By then I'd learned
that a body could carry
most memories forward
as things blown, breathe
out scars festering hot as
any day when standing
still could make shoes
melt. After he took my
pulses, felt pain surface
from my body through
needle-ends beneath his
own skin he blew it out
in one long breath. He
called it near enough to
death. He said, you will
have to go on living now.

IN CALIFORNIA

When the mother Hass
avocado tree died &
they put out the bid

for makers to make
something out of it
my brother sent photos

of beautiful pieces made
out of sister- or brother-,
or maybe even its father-

wood. He didn't
do it to please anyone
but himself, just wanted

to work that tree, find out
what she was made of. When
he couldn't say for sure what

he would create, or how long
it would take, or how much
it would cost, it was like

they were lost. So, in his
community garden in L.A
turns out there's at least

a couple old avocado trees
even better than Hass die
every year. He works them

where they lie.

BIRTHDAYS

Born twin, 8th of May 1959,
Los Angeles, same day cops
dragged out one remaining

resident of Chavez Ravine—
it's always a woman last
to leave— for demolition

after eviction of American
citizens, descent Mexican,
whose claims to land &

neighborhood did not
stand a chance to white
ownership, to the whims

of a white baseball-team's
owner from Brooklyn to
relocate large, stadium big

as communities that stick
together until colonized
by the very next robber

rides in on a copter
pointing finger down
to new site for games,

profit, mountains tamed
& flattened by machines
for a level playing field,

parking lots, for real-
estate with a view & free
of poverty, brown people

displaced from foothills
& free of fare-dodgers
gave the team its name.

Later, same city, we played
over-the-line with bat & ball
but no field in the middle

of streets, dodging traffic
& learning how to hit
& throw a straight

line. It happens
all the time: woman
always last to leave

the wreckage, broken
homes & people making
way for nothing but some

one else's field of play.

ENDURANCE TEST

Mr. Warner
told us
to stand
on our heads
until only one
of us was left
upside down.
For two hours
arms shook,
abdominal
muscles held
then cramped
& student after
student gave
up & fell to a
padded floor
we called, gym.
Until it was
just two of us:
one boy who
would do any
thing to win
which meant,
survive, & the
other, who I'm
guessing now
just wanted to
know he was
alive though
I don't even

remember his
name. I might've
stood on my head
all day, into night,
no matter pain
or hunger, such
was my drive
simply to get by
until I realized how
futile the exercise
had become two
boys outlasting all
predictions, one
unknown to
the rest of us.
So I gave in,
finally, let him win
assume the mantle
of longest lasting
head-stand in school
or maybe human
history, who knows—
just the two of us—
his record's safe with me.

ONE OTHER QUESTION

Celia asked if she could go
to the bathroom & Mrs.
Glenn, who doubted all
such requests, said, no, &
that might have been it if
Celia hadn't asked again,
this time more urgently,
& if Mrs. Glenn hadn't
said for the second time
but with a singular lack
of patience, no!, &, so by
the time Celia stood up
to go anyway our 2nd
grade teacher had lost
her grip entirely, anger
obscuring vision so the
drip of yellow urine on
Celia's chair wasn't even
clear to her, I swear
I could feel the heat of
shame, the warm seat,
the wetness on cheeks,
Celia leaving the room
to Mrs. Glenn's scream
telling her not to come
back, & all these years
later, me, sitting here,
needing to go, & asking,
because tyranny wants
to be answered, finally,
what could I have done?

DRILL

The teacher said to get under our desks,
crouch down as if in prayer & place
our hands behind our necks.

It was a weekly drill: what to do
in case of sudden nuclear war. Our
teacher said we should be perfectly

still, &, also, closed the door. As I
curled my body into position on
the cold, dirty floor, I felt safer

than I did at home, where explosions
of a different kind were a daily
occurrence. Here there was talk

of deterrents, having more bombs
than someone else, how these
would prevent consequences

we wouldn't be able to defend
ourselves against. A bell rang
to signal all clear, but I knew

I was still going home that night,
no saving desk in sight.

AT THE ROLLER SKATING RINK
for Linda

He holds my sister's hand
as if he wants to be her father,
but he doesn't.

Her dress hand-sewn
by our mother when
she did that kind of thing,

this woman who said, no,
to buttons, patches, &, sew
your own damn hems.

My sister looks as happy
as a girl can look who's about
to lose her mom.

For many years neither
one of them will know
what to make of this.

TIME, WEEK ENDING: 1994

after a Print by Tony Askew

A year time-tables seemed to change
every month, became changing
tables preparing for a diaper to come,

then two at a time, then three, that little
-over-a-year of conspicuous conception,
our life reduced to welcoming each new

moon as if we deserved it, asking where
time went, one moment leaves firing
before they dropped two more eggs

as easily as into a heated pan, over
easy, but also hard as hospitals so
many of us are born in & return to

so no surprise we feel both first & last
the fear of arrival, time, week ending:
1994, a genocide in Rwanda began &

Nelson Mandela was sworn in we
wondered if we could juggle twins,
holding on for dear life, while yet

another egg considered a drop, only
just fingering cracks that would later
lead her to a family where time had

become relative— nine months + ten
months equaling three kids bellying
up out of time beginning in 1994 a

federal judge ruling that the state
of California could not deny basic
services to illegal immigrants, &

asking ourselves all the time about
bringing more lives into this world,
 thinking, well maybe just one, both

of us bad at math of basic biology
which turned out to be incalculable,
indecipherable, newspaper headlines

all in Kanji & Japanese lady-
bugs covering walls & ceilings
where it had been printed

as prophesy a week
ending & beginning
 in time, in 1994,

still other lives
ahead of us &,
also, them.

FIRST SNOW

So soft even dogs
stop barking, cities'
edges blur into nothing,

streets lose dividing
lines, & no one wants
plows or shovels coming

anytime soon. We have
a foot by noon. Family's
already furrowed: not

one of us needs to do
anything except be in
this cocoon brought on

by weather that postpones
suddenly unimportant
things we were meant

to do, meetings, errands.
This day is for writing
letters, making soup,

putting jig-saw puzzles
together, even though
we've done them all at

least a hundred times.
It's fine being here,
just the five of us, in

this remote place
now that snow's
taken us off

the map. I go
upstairs, read,
take a nap. It

all goes
on with
out me.

III

THE ETIQUETTE OF GREEN

after Frank O'Hara

Pine needles find out
the color of my eyes
& deepen them: thin

leaves pricking air &
working it like some
tailor of space, cuff-

ing, folding, dressing
or simply sewing a
seam, liminal, be-

tween worlds, ways
an acupuncturist
finds points in a

body, energy al-
most dashing one
place to another,

any scent upwind
finding noses of
all the creatures

discerning enough
to read between
those thin lines

in search of food,
prey, & predators
pinned in place,

stilled by what all
senses have taken
in, so much green

I've turned mossy,
while each & every
creature still smells

I'm here.

TODAY, CLIMBING THE ROCK-FACE
for Margaret

heart announces itself deep in chest's
bass-line, keeping time, percussion
just another rhythm to go with breath,
steps, eyes moving from down, toward
toe-hold, to up, to the top of this climb
I might have run up when I was young
& did not know my limits. Now, tuned
into a missing string or two, I play my
fingers raw with less, press my index
& middle finger to my wrist noticing
hard pulse of exertion, arrhythmic
pauses or down-beats where before
the only thumps were regular, routine,
when knees did not balk, when talk
was about everything except sharp
rise, steep movement toward some
old accomplishment made newer
with age. & even noticing we're on
the same page, my lover & I, savor-
ing each moment of this slower
ascent, too hot, having not brought
enough water, blisters biting up
through skin. It doesn't matter
what shape we're in, whether or not
we make it all the way to the top, al-
though, today, it is worth noting, we
will. What matters is each step she
takes ahead of me & the way it draws
me like a rope, pulls me up toward
all of our years together, climbing.

THE DAY OUT OF TIME
for Audrey Lopez

First, dog named Sirius, rises
with the sun, stretches, shines
in a star worth thirteen moons.

Call it a day of realignment to
the non-human, free, fully off-
calendar, a liminal space after

any gestation, the brief pause
that might contain new life
beyond this one, all the laws

of our life experience held
in the feminine, 260 days,
give or take, until another

birth. But don't get ahead
of yourself. First, the dog
who is also a star rises on

twenty-fifth day of the
seventh month, yawns
or longs out a fourth

dimension, eternal
time, where any-
might happen

& then does.

THESE DAYS
for Martín Prechtel

Ants cross kitchen counters
& sugar trails designed to lead
them out before a woman I love

commits ant-genocide seem only
to invite them to linger longer so
that my own attempt to spare

their lives becomes another kind
of murder. Ants! you say, as in,
just, because maybe small scale

diminishes sentience. I can't help
telling you the story of a man who
built a large mud-house not before

moving all of the ant-hills around it
to offer ants something in return.
Mutual indebtedness he called it.

I can't remember just now what
he offered them but I suppose
it was something better

than sugar. Meantime, I'm apt
to argue a hill's home, too, that
scale has nothing to do with it,

that talk of humans' smallness
fills oceans. Dolphins can't stop
laughing at our lack of humility,

even as they leave trails of krill
for us to follow into the Pacific.
To date they haven't swept any

humans away, but tsunami's do
as a matter of course & maybe
that's worth noting, how earth's

plates shift under pressure, cause
dramatic undulations on ground
we walk on. Everything falls back

down to where it started:
ants wait for whatever
they can carry many

times their weight on their backs
home. &, *Sugar,* I say, *just this once,*
why don't you just leave them to it?

NIGHTS

After workdays it's time to get after it, mind
buzzing about like that creature burying
its head in some sweetness before emerging

with what it needs to spread the wealth, which
is to say, growth, pollen a currency we
cannot live without. Now all the talk's about

collapsing hives, pesticides come back
to haunt & most nights my mind's
no longer tuned to the hum of purpose

as if the drone under everything stopped
being audible. I'd say we're in trouble
if I knew what the trouble was, chemicals,

& climate change or a world that's lost
its queens. Either way there's sure to be
another night of wakefulness, when real

work gets done while
others toss & turn
in their forgetfulness.

LOVE POEM

Smaller than crook
when dog has folded
up his body coiled
for sleep, this pocket
of time big enough
to smell, say some-
one else's breath
before a kiss, one
you could miss if
you're not careful—
years of counting
(on) them, this daily
turn into waking
that makes of love
a tiny, tender thing.

THE WEATHER

Long before severe
dementia, aphasia,
before words lost
their connection
to thinking, even
sentences, mother
liked most talking
about weather, say
sudden cold snaps
that, in LA, meant
under 65 degrees
or, in all the other
countries, 18.3, &
how hot it was &
not even summer!
When she finally
had a house with
air-conditioning,
she kept it meat-
locker cold, said
put on a sweater
to my father if he
complained. You
don't even need
a refrigerator,
I said, just keep
perishables in
the bathroom,
& she laughed,

kept icy air
coming. All the
rest of us stayed
outside as much
as possible made
of the backyard a
whole house.
Now that
she no longer has
a house, my mom
still keeps rooms
in memory care
units cold as she
can.

caregivers
& visitors wear down
jackets & though
she doesn't
remember how to
swim or walk or
talk she keeps up
a steady stream
& at times even
seems to tread
in water
like she once did,
saying, so what's
the weather like
out there? Cold

I bet? & though I
ignore the fact
that we no longer
live "out there"
where it snows on
the east coast,
I say, well, it's still
not as cold as
your house, & both
of us laugh so
hard it might have
melted something.

COLLAGRAPHIC

My father
the rock hound
discovered a way
to drill down far
enough to see a
few fossils he knew
were there & also
knew something
about the fuels
made from them,
looked away from
futures dangerously
flammable. He
showed us countless
snail-shell spirals held
in rock, fish-bodies
flattened by weight
of centuries of earth,
bones of creatures so
old they resisted any
kind of recreation,
even imagined ones.
He told us his hands
were buried far down
& dirt-deep into both
geo & anthro secrets
& that they would,
with any bit of luck,
bring back stories
to be told again.
Meantime

he never could
wash blood or
oil off his hands
no matter how
hard he tried;
meantime fires
began to burn
so hot surfaces
of land started
to liquefy a new
lava.
Even then
he could feel all
of it turning in
on itself, layers
of shale folding
like origami—
creased,
combustible.

COUNTING TO THREE

while holding my mother's
hand in flame, her mother's
way of telling her to stop

touching the stove, & my
mother did stop, & took
stock of the learning, too,

started to write a book on
mind over matter. One day
I returned from next door

after Russell's dad beat up
his mom & told her about
it & she said, Ricky, don't be

so unpleasant; go outside &
play; it's sunny. & I did,
but only after looking, 1

more time at her own
scarred fingertips, my
mind unable to pass

that other
thing that
mattered.

WHERE I'M FROM

Santa Ana winds blew
over mountains & also

set fire to them, so whole
summer days we breathed

ash into our lungs sparked
by hottest blast of air

we'd ever felt. Smog was
daily, particulate, that

slight hurt at the bottom
of our breathing, but

nothing's ever knocked me
flat as those winds coming

over the mountains, fueling
the fire of my boyhood,

like a fever I would
never leave behind.

SOUNDS
for Margaret

Nights here owls call out
in coastal pines, waves

sound their nearness,
swallows rustle in their

nests under eaves. Most
mornings Mexican sage's

purple flowers vibrate audible
drones from bees & humming-

birds, & a sweet dog wakes
to first light, shakes his own

body in order to break into
our sleep. After that, he

paws the side of the bed.
If I'm lucky I've woken

ahead of him listened
to your breathing

in sleep or dreams. I hold
onto that sound same way

I always have, not taking
anything for granted, not

children with whom we've
nested, not this hum, not

the sound of waves always
or the calls of owls asking,

who? All these years
of waking to your breath

in, out, in & out,
it has always been you.

STILL-LIFE WITH RAIN
for Zebith

10 pm, herniated disc,
doctor's orders to walk
even if takes hours just
to stand upright. You're
thinking there's nothing
like night-stalking

sidewalks of a suburb,
so inside the box for an
entomologist-illustrator,
outside so human, man-
icured even wild keeps a
kind of order,

predatory habits hidden
from view, domesticated,
mostly on the down-low,
you are thinking, since
thinking is all you have
these days, prone

or sitting for stretches
in pain so bad it turns
rings around you. Yes,
hidden from view, you
say again, lawns, trees,
bushes signing

humans, just a stray
weed or two, the likes
of you, more creature
than human, far too
human to be any less
than creature.

Then, at your feet, a
writhing in slick rain,
&, not thinking now,
bent to hands & knees
you see four slugs tied
to courting,

suburban sod not close
to thwarting their slow
rituals toward love. You

know you won't last
long yourself hands
& knees observing

this dance & have
already lain down
on your good side,

head in hand, eyes
pointed down to
more passion than

you have ever been
part, privy to, two
of them curving

body over body
glued together
by silk trails

they also
leave be-
hind.

You're so
done in
you don't
even note
cars passing
slow to see
if woman
lying in
sidewalk
rain is al-
right, if
she's in
need of
help, &
slugs so
absorbed
in each
other
no one

notes
you,
1/2
wild
in ab
sorb
ing
what
you
are
see
ing.

This close-up you are thinking nothing
looks like it used to, not sidewalk, not
slugs in their mating dance, not cars
sliding on rain-slicked roads, skidding
to stops asking after your wellbeing.

How do you explain you are seeing
passion in its own good time, slower
time-based release into who knows
what? Sensual? That word does not
begin to describe this spaciousness

inside the box, square of sidewalk,
spot of light, slime trails leading to
love like of which you may never see
again? How to explain you might
not be able to rise after long minutes

of watching, rapt, attentive, back
seizing up again like human backs
do, leaving you alone, disappointed,
unsatisfied as a slug sliding solo on a
night it meant to send hermaphroditic
energy into another body, to find (out
or in) the only other life it will ever know?

OUTSIDE ASWAN

roasted chicken sat out all day
in simmering heat & I felt sure
I'd suffer from eating it, spoiled,

looking down at countless flies
but someone with nearly nothing
to spare prepared this chicken &

now offered it to me before feeding
her own family, stirred by nothing
but kindness to offer food first to

a stranger, one who almost choked
on the blessing, thinking of germs,
something gone bad enough to turn

his stomach before generosity of spirit
unprecedented in his life to that point
announced itself to him. Stranger, no

longer, to myself, I ate, for once at
last fortified, well fed, fuller than
I'd ever been before.

AS IN, HAPPY
for Farai

Fierce even in play
baboons filch food
left by those who
do not know how
to pay attention.

Social, terrestrial,
females connect
to communities
for life, raise babies
together while males

move on, alone, maybe
to mate elsewhere, mark
their places & time with
new groups of females
before, again, losing

interest. Lonely boys,
haven't you always just
wanted a where to fall
into? Like all the rest
of us you will have

to let go of legacies
rooted to restlessness,
unsatisfied, unsettled
in family you've found.
There are morsels all

around you, not stolen
leftovers of happiness
only on the ground
of new lives, countries,
food moving from hand

to mouth. Move & stay,
choose both: grab after
this good moment be-
fore heading south.

I WORRIED

less about the fact of waking up
& more about staying awake,
taking more time each day

to taste volcanic earth back
of my tongue, tart berries
when they were young that

became green beans, &,
after fire, dark, roasted,
fit for hot water, a little

filtering, coffee. We call it
a break at the office, moving
from one cup to another,

as if our day can be made better
by that kind of waking. I started
to worry that maybe I was taking

what the world was offering in
that volcanic soil as a kind of
jolt just to get through

my day, collecting pay by toil
with benefits without actually
being of benefit. I worried

a lot back then about whether
or not my work mattered, my
thoughts scattered with or, as

it turned out, without caffeine.
Once you become suspicious
of yourself there's no going

back, your previous train
of thought's gotten entirely
off-track, & you begin to think

too much about that first fact,
of waking up, of making that first
cup of coffee, of wondering what,

today, you are going to do
with all that time you used
to have.

IV

WHAT YOU MISSED
for Margaret

By this afternoon they'd
taken away all kitchen
tools, chairs, beds, even
tents that made others

at home in the houseless
encampment just down-
hill from our house. So
well hidden behind brush

only people who live here
knew they were there &
I figured most all of us
didn't care seeing as how

they'd been out there for
a while, off & on close to
a year, weather allowing,
& it did, most of the time.

I can tell you this morning,
though, off-leash, our dog
didn't go there to scavenge
after leftovers as if he knew

something was about to go
wrong, & also that mourning
doves' song sounded more
lonely than usual in trees

that were a natural canopy.
Later, Anne listened while
I told her why I didn't like
the word, incest, domestic

to my ear, too safe back
there in somebody's idea
of family. where worst
things aren't supposed

to happen to you. This
is no ordinary love
poem. Except that I
still want you to know

everything, even hard
stuff, like those people
losing their shelters no
matter how many others

see it differently; also,
homes we're born into
that are no safer than
materials they went up

with: silica, mud, wood;
how unprotected some
of them are: a change
in weather or nearness

to rage-range bringing
them down. It's not like
those people without all
their things can now just

go to town, this village
others call, paradise,
but only if you have
the money to afford it.

Not that many, even
of them, can afford
beach-front though
those people nearby

encamped could hear
waves at night, owls
in coastal pines, same
as us. Us, who have

found such good luck
in this small house
with a son & a golden
dog who also live here.

It's safe at night, even
I know that, though I
still wake up most of
the time. Those times

he took most of the stuff
I held most close, near
harbored in the hidden
body I learned how to

disappear from to a much
safer place, not family, to
a tribe of fellow dissociates
waiting in the wings with

doves, ready to take flight
at any moment they might
come. & hopeful of staying
while being held in & by

the right hands, these, &
no ordinary love in no
ordinary love
poem.

PANDEMIC BOOKENDS

Back to front, a mother
dying without enough
oxygen even to see her
own way out, solstice,

darkest day of the year.
Unless that was a year
ago, a father fighting
it out at closing just as

alone. Each of us loses
another parent & now
also knows how it feels
to step up to new states

as elders, which, maybe
among other things, =
next, next in line, next
near enough to say what

it feels like nearing end-
time, next launching
place or person or spirit
-filled land, beginning

long or short descent
into the unknown, &
both dreading, longing
to know what comes—

NOT QUITE TWILIGHT

wipe away tears

that come from
remembering

she can not
remember

anymore, that
this is now

her life.

•   •   •

They call it memory
care on the memory

care unit, but not
one person has ever

remembered how
to give up ghosts

they do not know
they've left behind.

MY MOTHER, DYING WHILE WALKING THROUGH DARKNESS TOWARD LIGHT ON THE WINTER SOLSTICE

for my mother, born Alberta May Fuller, 1ˢᵗ of May 1930

on the 21st of December, this year
of no lord, 2020, when most every
leader failed to lead, or did so very
badly, my mom waited all day until
someone finally showed up in ICU
whose voice she recognized to tell
her it was time to go. When you
have severe dementia someone
needs to tell you when to go, say,
we love you & now you can loosen
your life-grip & there's nothing &al
so no one else you need to live your
life for any longer, &, so long, you'll
be missed. When you've forgotten
everything it goes unnoticed by
you that it's the shortest day
of the year, & the darkest,
but you still choose not
to leave until knowing
it's going to stay a
little lighter
tomorrow.

How does someone
who has lost more
than her mind even
come to know this?

No one knows how
the soul does it, not
even the soul, who,

by the way, doesn't
go by that name.

All the same, I swam
laps for you today,
mom, at the small
pool down-street,
where, if you angle
it just right it can
feel like a lane to
someplace worth
going to, thought
well of you & re
membered to ex
press gratitude,
even for things
you did badly
but also best
way you knew
how, & now
my arms &
legs are tired

& it's
going
to be
a little

lighter
today
but I
guess
already

you know that.

(AMERICA NEVER WAS AMERICA TO ME),
after Langston Hughes

but it was to you?
& him, too? Who

am I to say what
was, wasn't, or,

for that matter
what is or isn't

true? I will say
nothing's new,

that freedom's
just for a chosen

few, also that it
won't do, this

promise long
past due, & so

many singing
the blues, bop,

Bach & Bessie
too. You, me,

then America
will be.

(TO WHAT WE BEAR
WITNESS IS OUR STORY TO TELL)
in memory of Daunte Wright

She is just out of Greek
tragedy central casting

& he, he's stuck in a role
she thinks she's already

seen him play: black man
stopped by police which's

also to say, her, woman
among men for twenty-6

some odd years made to
do scut-work; she's never

even fired her gun, tazer,
always gets stuck with a

new trainee still trying to
show she's just as good a

cop as any man, when she
maybe sees an expired tag,

not illegal, but also an air-
freshener hanging from a

rearview, which is. His re-
cords clean she's shocked

to see: after all he's a black
man, but she's got the lead

(she's with the trainee) &,
soon enough she's a white

woman in charge among a
gaggle of white men all of
them hell-bent on getting
him out of his car because

of an air freshener hanging
on the rearview. How he's

used that same mirror, dbl-
consciousness, watching all

assemble round his car. He
already knows that he can't

take this injustice too far,
but he sure as hell isn't

getting out of this car
seeing as containment

of terror's the only play
he's got,

Ma'am? so much courtesy
in the middle of rough &

rude, he can tell she's no
good, too, just another one

of the guys, & also, already,
there'll be no wise or reason

for what
comes next:

another black man
driving,

while dead.

LOOKING AT A MURDER OF CROWS

Look long enough & you notice
they're in the family way, one's
calling the shots, another's

asking after food. A third's
so focused on preening (is
it his?) black-blue feathers

I think he might be vain:
me, who hates mirrors,
& him, & this constant

bustling into life.

SUB-LOGIC
for Walt

On the nuclear submarine one man had a job to push
a button upon orders from a general who would receive
his orders from a politician to deploy a nuclear war-head,
& another man already had orders that were also his job-
description to kill the first man for failing to follow through.

These men had spent six months together on the submarine
in close quarters deep under the Baltic Sea near Helsinki, &,
more to the point, Moscow, & both of them, even on brink
of friendship, knew the score. Because this was during the
Cold War, no matter how deep already the drink of their

intimacy they had to follow orders. Far from adding a sort
of chill to a friendship, it plumbed to the bottom of their
hearts—none of this was going to end well: if one died his
friend would have been through the hell of pulling them
apart, not to mention, after pulling the trigger, pushing

a button that would change the world. Just to be safe,
there was a countdown, lasting two minutes, between
decision & deployment. Twice already it had begun & a
politician had to tell a general who told the submarine
commander who told the two men it was a false alarm.

During those long moments both of them had ample
time to consider doing harm as well as following orders.
One believed in his country. The other had read Forster's
words, If I had to choose between betraying my friend &
betraying my country, I hope I would have the guts to

betray my country. Neither, I wish I could say, of course,
was ever charged with following orders. & neither of them
told my friend & me this story. It was their fellow soldier
said how it was after he'd had enough drink to spill States'
secrets. My friend, Walter, who'd served in the military

so knew how to follow orders, quickly said that, no matter
what, he'd have pulled the trigger & killed me. I said that
I was worried about false alarms, orders repealed too late
to keep the peace, of pledging allegiance to a country asking
me to make such decisions. Walter, who by then had saved

my life more than once said again that he'd not hesitate
to pull the trigger. But how would you figure in friendship?
& he said he wouldn't, couldn't: he had a job to do
& someone
had to do it.

I PREFER KEEPING A NEEDLE &
THREAD ON HAND
JUST IN CASE

a button loses its hold
on the other side of a

hole, a pair of pants
needs a patch at knee-

point, dish-rags ask
to made into small

drapes, discernable
fraying begins at the

napes of necks on
favorite shirts, or

flirting turns to
hurting in no time

& the heart needs
a stitch or two

just to keep its
off-beat twitch

from turning
into nervous

tics. The rest
I can't speak of

but it is also, of
course, nearer &

on hand when-
ever it's needed.

GRUNION RUN

During one, thousands
of silver-backs, as they're
sometimes called, click

bodies up-beach, moon
light making of it all
sharp percussion, pacific

sand become mercurial,
the spawning "runners"
you can only cup in your

hands, the law says,
during those two hours
of birthing & giving up

bodies at the same time.
There's actually a rule
says that it's a crime

to take more than 30
home with you, though
for enough grunion-

tacos to go around
you'll need way more
than that, &, anyway,

cops are here mainly
to break up the fights
that seem to happen

when crowds gather,
even those witness-
ing a miracle, sand

turning metallic &
liquid along length
of this coast, from

Mexico to California
knowing no borders
&, for once, no way

to keep them out,
from these beaches
where they give them

selves up for a next
generation, all that
commitment to a

few nights of con-
tinuation, sacrifice,
&, for us humans,

the spectacle, the
pulsing ground
vibrating birth &

death, &, finally,
a harvest, &, after
that, a feasting on it.

I PREFER NOT TO ASK HOW MUCH
LONGER & WHEN

Because there is something in simply opening
one's eyes each morning between sleep &
waking, because those first conscious breaths

into a new day are the also a first way
of making something happen, some
new act of creation that will also come

to define me. Because fate is a refusal
of surprise, change, of some new
becoming. Because to know what's

next is also like reading some sacred
text from the back-end first, my
sorry ass hanging in the balance

between what I've already learned
& don't yet understand & what's
now bound to happen whether or

not
I want
it, too.

OLD PILLOW

So flattened by weight, gravity
or loss of down or foam
it lay beneath my head no

softer than ground, so many
decades of seeing me to sleep
or not, toward good dreams

or nightmares or my hours
turning over days like compost
piles, all those nights becoming

many miles of a life so unsettled
it kept me awake half of the time.
Still, to me it was sublime, smell

taking me all the way back to my
college days & maybe even beyond
that, to boyhood, not best of times,

barely tolerable, yet I clung
to it as if it was something
loved. My older neck ached

for something comforting,
sleep-inducing, tuned to a
life I had grown into. I got us

both new pillows. You traded up,
while I put mine on top of the one
I might have left behind, replaced

but not gone, ghost-ground, so
slight in the way of padding for
these fewer years I had ahead.

STILL LIFE WITH CITY STREET & LIQUOR STORE

By late middle-ages dead ends
of childhood surface like bad
dreams, half-remembered,
that September Santa Ana
winds blew in so hot & dry
they seemed to spark fire all
by themselves, no match or
half-lit cigarette thrown out
of a passing car required.
Tonight's window opens
to sidewalks' simmer close
to boil, shimmering out in
air-waves kindred to water
& sun's so bright words
come out of nowhere to
shadow sides of buildings:
lost our lease; quality liquors
& spirits, 40's half off while
supplies last. Those days
no one on my block drank
anything but Coors or Bud.
We hugged our bodies fetal
under-desk to protect our
selves from nuclear bombs.
Everywhere we looked some
shadow spelled out, The End.

SEEING IN THE DARK

Under-house between foundation
& earth, maybe two feet, just small

& big enough for two twin boy-
bodies to squirm through dirt,

snake-like, in order to find three
desert tortoises sleeping out winter

as if they might not possibly be able
to withstand it otherwise. I do still

hear your cries, as dirt & dust filled
your ears & eyes, how our escape

from the brutalities we could still
hear overhead would never amount

to sleep, even forgetfulness, living
through another season in a strange

place we called, family. Once, two
tortoise elders, thought well beyond

the age to do so, conceived a child
& we watched in awe that spring,

of that mild upbringing, until, for
some unknown reason, it simply

died after several months. When
a father lifts life out of its element

& transports it to a city, life some-
how adapts, does the best it can,

finds solace in burrows beneath
a house. But of course they know

it's not a desert floor they've
found their way to & maybe

it's not even possible to seed
new life in the terms of such

containment. We witnessed
all of them die or disappear in

the end, just as you did, dear
brother, for over twenty years,

until you came back, to me,
to us, as if the ground be-

neath you had been solid
all that time. Maybe some

crime had been committed,
maybe not. This dust-filled

story of us & desert tortoises
is more or less all I've got.

BETWEEN TWO CANYONS
ON AN AUGUST AFTERNOON
for John Davis

Barely trail underfoot, how
locals like it, we follow a
trace of sand between

river & two red walls
worn smooth, nearer
to cliff-dwellers 5,000

years old even if they
have also been gone
that long. Anything

noticed or witnessed
calls us back through
time. Some others

dropped twine-braided
ropes & people down
vertical rock-face in

order to carve out
a place they could
feel safe sleeping

recessed into heart
of stone far enough
out of reach of those

who would come
all this way just
to harm them.

River-rock cuts
our bare feet
once we've

lost the trail,
figuring water's
as good a path

as any. Scratches
from brush &
sharp-tipped

branches dry
red on faces
in sun, & turkey-

vultures over-
head smell blood
& begin to feel like

no joke. A mile ago
the way ran clear
enough, & getting

lost between walls
& a slow-running
river pulling us in

a non-negotiable
line, unlikely.
But it's fine to be

a little lost again
in red sand so
heavy in shoes

our noisy knees
& backs begin
to feel the weight

while we follow
no trace of a trail
back to where we

started hours ago,
no sign that we
ever set out. One

store-room up-
cliff could once
have served as a

watchtower
& someone
might have

watched us:
old enough
to leave it

all alone.

CODA

CREDO

after Alicia Hokanson

I believe in early-morning
dolphins feeding on krill
at the wave-line,

in oatmeal, hot, in early
spring, I believe

in quiet talk first thing
before the day's

turned to the many
wars, to the people

now living without
ceilings, doors, & to

the people already
living without them,

in hearts that reach
toward any seed or

root worth growing
& I believe in

knowing that comes
with the fruit

of your labor, in
what even a tongue

can savor, &, often,
does. I believe

in this morning
waking up, same

as always near you,
in our spoon-to-

spoon clinging
gently to this life

without needing
too much from it

&, in gratitude,
gratitude.

ACKNOWLEDGMENTS

Some of these poems have appeared in the following journals and magazines, sometimes in slightly different versions; my gratitude, as always, to the editors and publishers:

"Pandemic Bookends" and "(America Never Was America to Me") in *The Independent*

"Old Pillow" & "if something should happen" in *While You Wait* (an anthology edited by Laure-Anne Bosselaar and published by Gunpowder Press

"How to Make Santa Ana Wind" and "A Report on the Weather" in *Fledgling Rag*

"Still Life with City Street & Liquor Store" in *Elsewhere Paradise* (an anthology curated by the Sullivan Goss Gallery (paintings by Patricia Chidlaw) & edited by Enid Osborn)

"Late Storm," "These Days," "Saving's," "if something should happen," "Candle-pod Acacia," and "Day Outside of Time" in *The Wayfarer*

"The Etiquette of Green" and "Counting to three" in 10 Anniversary Anthology of *The Wayfarer*

"I prefer not to use a needle & thread" in *The Woolf*

"Time— Weekending, 1994" *Santa Barbara Printmaker's Show* (after a print by Tony Askew)

"I prefer to knock on wood," & "I prefer not to ask how much longer & when" in *Wislawa Szymborska: a Bookmaking Project* by Kelly Steben at CCA

"Fig Tree in a Fallen City" in *Poetry is Bread* anthology (ed. Tina Cane)

I am grateful, as always, to Les Browning and her skillful editorial staff at Homebound publications, and to my friend and colleague, Abby Lazerow, for the use of her fine painting on the cover of this book, *Domestic Terror*. Martín Prechtel continues to inspire me with his teachings, and, no doubt, they have found their way into this poetry. My daughter, Sarah Jewell Benjamin—poet, teacher—read and commented on every page of this book. A bow in her direction.

ABOUT THE AUTHOR

Rick Benjamin lives on unceded Chumash land in Goleta, California, and walks each day on indigenous trails. He teaches courses at the University of California Santa Barbara, among them poetry and community, the wild literature of ecology, and literatures of both social and juvenile justice, while also working among elders, young people at a local Boys and Girls Club, in art museums and youth detention facilities. Among his other works are the books of poetry, *Passing Love, Floating World, Endless Distances,* and *Some Bodies in the Grief Bed,* and his next book of poetry. He served as the poet laureate of Rhode Island from 2012 – 2016.

HOMEBOUND
PUBLICATIONS

WAYFARER

BASED IN THE BERKSHIRE MOUNTAINS, MASS.

The Wayfarer Magazine. Since 2012, *The Wayfarer* has been offering literature, interviews, and art with the intention to inspires our readers, enrich their lives, and highlight the power for agency and change-making that each individual holds. By our definition, a wayfarer is one whose inner-compass is ever-oriented to truth, wisdom, healing, and beauty in their own wandering. *The Wayfarer's* mission as a publication is to foster a community of contemplative voices and provide readers with resources and perspectives that support them in their own journey.

Wayfarer Books is our newest imprint! After nearly 10 years in print, *The Wayfarer Magazine* is branching out from our magazine to become a full-fledged publishing house offering full-length works of eco-literature!

Wayfarer Farm & Retreat is our latest endeavor, springing up the Berkshire Mountains of Massachusetts. Set to open to the public in 2025, the 15-acre retreat will offer workshops, farm-to-table dinners, off-grid retreat cabins, and artist residencies.

WWW.WAYFARERBOOKS.ORG